GARDENING WITH DEER

KATHY MILES

INDEPENDENT INNOVATIVE INTERNATIONAL

Published by Cinnamon Press,
Meirion House,
Tanygrisiau
Blaenau Ffestiniog,
Gwynedd,
LL41 3SU
www.cinnamonpress.com
The right of Kathy Miles to be identified as author of this work
has been asserted by her in accordance with the Copyright,
Designs and Patent Act, 1988. Copyright © 2016 Kathy Miles.
ISBN: 978-1-910836-26-2
British Library Cataloguing in Publication Data. A CIP record for
this book can be obtained from the British Library.
Designed and typeset in Palatino by Cinnamon Press. Printed in
Poland. Cover design by Adam Craig
Cinnamon Press is represented in the UK by Inpress Ltd
www.inpressbooks.co.uk and in Wales by the Welsh Books
Council www.cllc.org.uk

Acknowledgements

Acknowledgements are due to the following publications,
in which many of the poems in this collection first
appeared:

*Interpreter's House, Envoi, ARTEMIS, Poetry Wales, The
Lampeter Review, Orbis, Planet, New Welsh Review, The Lonely
Crowd, Roundyhouse*, and anthologies published

Contents

Gardening With Deer

Bear

There's always a bear in the cave,
a breath in the slurred dark.
The smell of sweet fur thick as fear.
The prowl of wind against your face
your nostrils filled with bear
and the growl of night as you unhook
yourself from an old belief.

He is there when you look up
and see the trees so tall above the house
the breeze blowing leaf-fall on the soil.
He is there when you wake with a knot
of terror, in that early hour
when ice bitters a rim of glass
and the snarl of dreams is waiting.

Nothing is still
nothing is forever
a wasp brushed from hair
an insect punching the surface of the pond.
The wind in the trees, the growling dark
the shadow on the wall that could be bear.

The Woman and the Hare

She lies in moonlight, pale against white pillows,
watches through the window a flurry of falling stars,

the caught fall of acorns. Hears a brack of water
trickle down roof and gutter, a fret of air

in the branches. That brown nimbus of hair
is softened with grey at this year's turning,

but her gaze is as bright as when she slipped,
golden-eyed from the sac, into a hard indurate world.

She's cold all the time now, cold as stone,
as if her flesh was lined with frost, the veins

with runnels of ice, and she shapeshifts
into wool and quilt against the coming dark.

So the hare sitting in the field at dusk, her skin
bleached by earthshine, sees the red kite circle

a Neolithic sky, feels the sift of wind in her fur.
Bone-rooted to her land, she crouches

in ridged furrows of soil, nests in spurred
grasses and threshed stubbles of wheat.

Her running stopped, the swift thrust of her legs
slowed by the stalk of winter, brittle chill of hail.

What she has seen and known, remembered
in her shallow breath, the wane of blurred shadows,

a grief of crows in the trees. The glaze of her
stargazing eyes fixed firmly on an old mythology.

Gardening With Deer

And now you know for yourself how it is.
The ragged hours' breathing,
long nights and longer days.
Watching her shift in her sleep,
as the moon turns and skies alter
and the ghost-trees of early morning
are heavy with frosted leaves
like a fruit of hanging doves.

A lifetime of gardening with deer,
their rough noses huffing
over the fence, nipping at the roses.
Fraying the bark of saplings
to remove the velvet, their heads
laid against the trunks. The stag
whipping the branches with his antlers.

All this is remembered in a still room
where the spirit of the white deer
with an arrow in his heart
walks through her dreamtime,
and the sweet musky sigh of roebuck
in the back of her throat
rises with every breath.
You hold her hand,
anxious, yet dreading her waking.

Slate

In winter, this road would be a harsh drive.
The valley quickened with mist,
the culverts frozen. Fields fly past

like blown birds, childhood coming closer
with each mile, last rosebay hanging
to the margins. A slow graze of sheep,

the ewes loose and sullen, slumped beside verges,
cropping the flint grass, wandering beyond
known boundaries, their own lineage.

And above, wet quires of slate, rising
in steep cliffs, a slew of stone slipping to the track.
Blue-grey, *glas*, the colour of gull or merlin.

At this final stage the year is weary.
Only a flare of gorse on the bleak slopes,
the smell of mountains heathered into rain.

At the end of the journey you greet us,
frailer now, wary as a lamb, cast in that
caul of our friendship, our mutual past

bleating its shared memory. Like a mother
calling to her young, crying to the wind,
the lost newborn.   Fracturing my heart.

Giving Her Brahms

We spun the truth of it like sugar strands,
just as that morning water was glazed
by a craze of ice, but the pool feeling only
the wholeness of its own world,
newts and nymphs sealed from winter.

And when the litter of her words
was carried away like washed pebbles,
we pointed to early primroses
and she understood the language of colour,
the print of pollen on her fingers,
the taste of green and gold.

And when she endlessly looped through
our conversation, we gave her Brahms,
the pearl of the violin's tone
dropping a thin string of cadenzas
into air light as a spinet.

Once she asked, *Why is this happening?*
and we gave her the scent of carnations,
the touch of fur, the stroke of a hand.
Tapping her heart for an old wisdom
that her head no longer knew.

Ancestry

i.m. Alice Ashton, 1875-1930

Her name shimmers on my tongue, like a taste
I can't identify. Eighty five years gone,
and the pain of missing her shafts through my DNA.
A single picture, faded now. Framed by trees
and bracken, two children squinting at the sun.
Her hands are still. But I know how raw
and chapped the palms were, skin rough
from washing clothes on winter days.

I take the weight of her name into my mouth,
breathe in the word of her, all the pages
she might have been, reach down
and drag her up through the years,
her dark eyes ghosting my own.

If I gave back the features I have borrowed,
my mother would get the hair that never curls,
my father, this long and melancholy face.
But to you, Alice, I'd return
that shy glance at the camera's lens,
the quirky purse of lips, my awkward smile.

The quiet bleach of things. Centuries laid out
like sheets at night, a slow dissolve in moonlight.
The only record in the owl's wingbeat
as he soars over churchyards, the inscription
on each headstone etched into his soul.

And this is where I find you, Alice,
asleep between woodrush and thistle,
overgrown, forgotten,
except for that space in the grail of my head
where you are still waiting.

Irises

A May garden, the flowers unleashed,
perfect for my camera. And you, kneeling
on a foam mat, laughing. You lift your hands
towards me, warding off the shot, fingers
black with compost, knuckles taut and raw.

Later, you bring in armfuls of iris,
arrange them in the old white vase.
Loving their blue stiffness,
the trinity of petals curving to the anther,
the falls of vivid cobalt.

And later, when I let you down,
as daughters sometimes do, you were
there as mothers always are. Weeding
out the bad, nurturing the new, still
loving the core of me, bearing the stigma.

The Grammar of Land

She struggles through layers of words, dense
as blankets a mother would lay on a winter bed.
Snuggles into the known: *Bore da! Sut wyt ti*

She prefers the language of the earth,
delving into a cleft of soil, sticky
as apple-crumble on her skin.

She's digging up the planet. Chitting potatoes
on the sill to catch the sprouting light,
trenching them deep against a bruise of frost.

She loves the buried horizons of clay,
the looseness of leaf and humus
with its debris of spiders, needles, lichen.

A smutch of silt splashing from the trowel,
her fingers quilted with dark loam,
feeling the sough of wind in the trees.

Her hands the grammar of land, sifting, weeding,
as she scoops out the ground, lifts roots,
burrows through crust and mantle.

Down to *creigwelyau*, the bedrock,
the iron-nickel heart.
The start of it all, and the ceasing.

The Woman Who Became Bee

She knew she was changing. She started to buzz,
to drone on about flowers, became pollen-legged,

crazed for the scent of salvia, penstemon.
She rubbed her calves on petals, sank her tongue

into the long pink well of a foxglove,
saw a giant sheet of light from different eyes.

They had come suddenly. A swarm that surrounded
her in a cloud, until she was dense with bees,

a solid honeycomb, skin fuzzy as stubble, as they
entered her pores, colonised her like a new planet.

The swarm spread through her bones,
snuggled into her breasts, settled in the marrow.

They made honey from her cells, formed a cadre
in her head, fed on capillaries, and she hummed

as though she was a taut wire, trembling with tension.
She sucked the bees into herself, became hive,

as the queen in her womb moved and shifted,
shivered along the arteries and veins.

Now she dances light as an aphid on her thin,
too-many legs, drinks sweet gold mead,

soars across the garden on her four wings,
fears the quick stealth of badger and dragonfly.

Whilst under her heart a new queen emerges
like a phoenix from the ashes of herself.

Strange Journeys

I remember when my mother-in-law slipped
from the loosened sash-cord of the window,
flew from the ward and walked on Brighton Beach.

Dazed with sleep, legs dangling from the blue
hospital gown, she shimmied through the air,
surprised an owl below an improbable moon.

She tells how first she looped the room, saw
that intimate delicacy inside her shoes,
the fatty patch of spilt milk by the door.

As she grew more sure of her balance,
she ventured to the ceiling, ran her hands
over the greasy, top-of-cupboard dust,

looked down at herself drowsing on the bed,
shifting gently in a patch of starshine,
but different, she says, *as if it wasn't me.*

She tells how she slid through the narrow
window-gap, hasped open for the wind
to ruffle the must of sickness and wasted air.

Wheeled with seagulls across the channel,
felt the keen whet of winter night,
the cryogenics of ice on her burning skin.

Floating down, she says, she saw the pier
stretched like a white arm in the darkness,
landed on sand, the gritty shingle's scrape.

Nestled back in bed, her face is flushed,
her temperature shooting to the skies.
Her hands fashion scrimshaws from the sheets,

and her breath is a ragged wave,
breaking unevenly on the groyne
of the bleeping green machines.

*I was walking on the sho*re, she says,
fretful and insistent. *Look at my soles,
how dirty they are, how grazed with tiny stones.*

They stroke her forehead with its thin wimple
of light, smooth her confusion of brown curls,
draw covers over her sea-bound legs

with their coating of salt. Clip back the wing-buds
on her shoulders, that threaten to sprout
coverts when they are not looking her way.

I take her hand, open it out like a moonflower.
Trace the lifeline that has nearly run out,
gently wipe the sand from her moistened palm.

A Building of Rooks

Tonight the rooks are trying to come in. I see them
fiddle with the chimney-cowl, slip through
rafter and fascia, steal along the gutters.

They chip at the brick, slowly deconstruct
the mortar. Joists creak alarmingly
above beams and ceilings at the gable end.

They murmur to each other from dark corners,
peck wantonly at pieces of cement, gloat over
beads of silicone sneaked away in their beaks.

Under my bed, dust rustles with glossy feathers.
Sheets lose their smoothness. Birds bounce together
on the duvet, carefully examine the Seiko clock.

Downstairs they are thimbling the silver, flicking
through my books. They preen themselves in front
of the mirror, leer across the room at me, press

against my mouth for a stolen kiss. They filibuster
round the house, drawn by lure of fridge and larder,
swagger like yeggmen onto the verandah.

Beaks pry into drawers and cupboard spaces,
peer inquiringly round the kitchen door,
gorge from the fruit-bowl on the dining table.

Relaxing on the back of chairs and settle,
they sit by the fire recounting ancient fables.
Peck out little morsels of my soul.

Garden Dragon

I bought him for his dragon-ness,
his sleepy stone eyes and watchful claws.

In winter he will glaze with ice, his still
wings stiffen, the scorch of his nostrils chill.

Now he wears autumn on his back, chipped
by bitter wind, scales grey with the season.

His bones so cold, so fragile, I could cup my hands
around them, myth him to life with my fingers.

The Girl With Pre-Raphaelite Hair

Her hair was a minefield
in which combs got lost,
exploded knots and tangles
when she brushed it.
Birds disappeared in her locks,
made nests, laid eggs, reared their young.
Bees were mislaid, and reappeared
in frightened swarms when she washed it.

Buzzards flew over her, watching
for the nuzzle of mice in her curls,
for the scuttle of baby rabbits.
Marigolds grew in careless blooms,
roses rampaged in her auburn maze,
flourished on strawberry shampoo.

Other girls envied her tresses,
ringlets cascading to her tiny waist.
But amorous swains with enquiring fingers –
rashly brave from the thrill of the chase
and brashly uncoiling at their peril –
found tendrils wound round their hands,
strands twisting along bare arms, and fled,
afraid of the tightening quill of hair.

At night whilst she slept in bed
it crept over the red silk duvet,
snaked away into dark corners,
behaved like no hair should.
For this was brave hair, hair with guts,
devious hair. Not womanly or decorous,
but wild, untamed, capricious.
Wilful and dangerous, like the girl
it had chosen to be its owner.

The Gift

She took it in both hands.
Examined it to see its colour, the quality,
what she might expect of it.
A surprise, she said, but still she smiled,
pale against the whiteness of the bed,
the wrapping from her present scattered
like a phial of pills on the floor.
The air smelt of red carnations,
and something else, something sweeter.

Her breath was a pearl in the hot room,
a slipstream too slight to stir a bee's wing.
And the flowers were difficult,
competed with her for the sliver of air.
Her hands fussed over the covers,
astonished fingers slid over silk.
And my gift, that small bequest I took back home
was the moment our fingers touched
and the air was brimming.

Pomegranate

Wind harrowing over rough scrub
scours the rim of withered grass.
On the pond the last thin strands of ice
like isinglass or angels' hair
thread between reeds and water lilies.

Collared doves peck for early seeds.
Squirrels pick at sour twigs
on the twisted pomegranate tree,
wanting sultry days of swelling buds,
bloom of shih liu in the fifth lunar month.

A girl sits in the kitchen
holding the hard shiny globe,
slices the skin with a sharp knife.
Red runs down her arms.
The flame of her hair like dangerous flowers,
her flesh, scented saffron.

In the hour of birds six silent seeds
slip from the split fruit. Cupped
in sweet aril, red as a hawk-cuckoo's tears.
The world changed, the earth barren
ground opening like a wound.
The sound of something breaking.

An Elegy for Lace

i.m. of the lacemakers of Chantilly, and the Sisters of Compiègne
(also lacemakers), executed in the French Revolution

In late afternoon, a tapestry of apples,
shadows stippled on the orchard's hem.

Scents of garlic and wild violet, the linnet
keening on the wind, a slur of sun in the grass.

A dragonfly, his wings stretched webs of thread,
rises in the bleach of evening dusk.

Our hands a quiet prayer of lace, inside
the honeyed stone of the cloister walls.

We loop the silky tussels of yarn, twist and plait,
cross them over and over, shape them

into shawls and veils, a fichu to be placed
round the neck of a comtesse or a queen.

Bone and ivory bobbins click like needles,
the clink of ships' masts at their mooring, as we link

meshed nets of grenadine across a réseau ground.
Each strip separate to itself, white as flaked ice,

our fingers raw from the prick of holding-pins.
The lark embroiders his song into our intricate work.

Yet the blet of sky darkens. Night cuts the earth
like a whetted blade. I grow afraid, Sisters, I grow so afraid.

The Lady and the Unicorn

Georges de Fournival, Journeyman Weaver, 1490

I wake with her face reflected in my head,
the rough draft of her cheek
the half-shaped cup of her chin,

and I'm impatient to begin my work.
She is woven into my breath, into
each heartbeat. Every day she grows

under my skilled fingers as I fill
the unformed landscape of her skin.
Here, the music of the loom purls through

the shed, creaks like a horse in his stall.
We string the heddles tight as a harp,
put the warp threads into the raddle,

set the tension right for an even weave.
We are deaf to the world, our hands raw
with the cut of wool, the stinging winter frost.

Today I'm gifting her a string of creamy
pearls, to be placed inside the casket held
by a chatelaine I have not crafted.

(For Antoine Serres has that task.
His lady is not so excellent as mine, her
features coarse, her dress a plainer *moiré*.)

At night I toss on the dark hours, see her
in my dreams. Imagine coiling her mouth
with scarlet, shadowing her eyes in plum.

I'd twist her lips with desire, put a beaded
pulse on the line of her cheek, so when I run
my hands along the ribbed warp-edge

I can almost feel it beating. But her eyes
are just for me. The lids heavy with pleasure,
the *hachure* of colours braided in her gaze.

For she is my Lady, *mon seul désir*. Already
I would fight lions for her, as I turn her slender wrist,
her shoulders' slope beneath the silk brocade.

And when she is finished, I would lie with her
in pansy and sweet rocket. In our senses, scents
of hyacinth and jasmine, her skin fresh

as strawberries, a plainchant of leaves
singing in the branches of the oak.
I would touch her outstretched palms,

take the jewelled pendant from her throat,
untie the narrow cord of her cabled belt,
unloose her hair from its stiff aigrette.

I would undo the unicorn stitch by stitch,
cut the warp-threads of his horn,
lie in her lap forever, courting her favour.

Collecting Fossils

Mary Anning, 1799-1847

1. A Girl Who Didn't Sew

I was never the sort of girl for sewing bees.
My seams clotted like buttermilk,
and pricked blood stemmed from my fingers
onto cretonne or fine-grained silk.

Not for me the quiet precision
of herringbone or chevron, the satin weave
of damask on a loom by candlelight,
turning the delicate cuff of a linen sleeve.

I wanted to be down on the shore,
scouring the shingle and seams of rock
for coprolites and crinoids, shells or quartz,
among the tumbled husks of dry sea-wrack.

I loved the intricate embroidery
of patterns interlaced within the schist,
the way a skull would suddenly appear
as if it had been stitched inside the cliffs.

My hands, that couldn't quilt or knit,
could ease a skeleton gently from the shale,
brush off the silt, lay out the broken spine,
the litter of ribs to make it whole again.

Only the beach would do, sand fine as muslin,
searching the slanted bias of the chert
for snakestone, brittle star or belemnite,
a secret curl of fossils in the dirt.

And when the shifting scarp unravels,
and boulders tumble to the ocean floor
I pray for grypheas, for pentacrinites,
to be dazed by the curdled eye of an ichthyosaur.

2. The Carpenter's Daughter
for Miriam

How could she resist?
The way the cliff parted its lips
to show bone, a sudden blench of jaw,
verteberries peeping from the flint.
Petticoats damp with the rush
and shuffle of small waves, crusted
with mud and salt, she sifted
the sediment for dragons' teeth,
for trilobites and urchins, the slender
graceful shape of a plesiosaur.

Sometimes, distracted by the living,
she'd see a scuttling hermit-crab,
shrimps skitter through a pool.
And she'd imagine them all dead,
all frozen in stone, and wondered, too,
how she would look: whether
her wide skirts would survive in blue lias,
and whether in two million years
her naked, indelicate bones
would be exposed by another's fossil hammer.

So now when I see you stride before
me on the shore, head down, absorbed,
your patchwork skirt brushing
the ridged sand, pockets full of pebbles,
quick eyes alert for ammonites,
I think of the carpenter's daughter,
chipping out a living from the rocks,
looking for snakestones in the shale.
For these silent creatures sleeping
in their unforgiving cradles.

The Red Shoes

I see her past go walking down the street
in its down-at-heel slip-shoe shuffle.

I remember how the wayward child in her
skipped off, bright as a geranium, in new red shoes,

a spinning, twirling sycamore. Her weight
lifting, then falling to the tarmac as she skittered

and hopped, avoiding cracks, free and light
as a swallow. In the churchyard she'd skim over

grass and plots, over tansy and sorrel,
over upturned faces deep below the earth

and they'd see her heels through the press of soil,
feel the vibration of her dancing. Now her shoes

are brown, sensible, solder her to a ground
that tries to shake her from herself. She lives the pain

through her feet, legs heavy as iridium, each step
a struggle as she jostles bags, a stumble of cobbles.

She wants shoes that will walk for her,
take off of their own volition.

Tap and flamenco her, take her flying
to mountain tops, up into the sky,

where she can glide and shimmy across the clouds,
slide along the burnished welt of stars.

Fox

He's asleep in her, nose cwtched up
to the red hollow of her mind.
He had stalked her through the dark scrambles
of wind, the restless winter midnights.
She saw him coming. That bright flash of fur,
the slight slur of ryegrass as he passed.
She wanted him, as a predator wants
the thrilled moment of chase and capture,
the soft crush of flesh in its mouth.
She longed for the purpose of him, that locking
of his eyes with hers, the whisper of his breath
on the snow. She dreams of him now.
Of tracking him through the tumble of her thoughts
always there, like a poem that stays with you forever.

Dark Matter

Even as I look, the stars are receding.
A grey January morning with its film
of cloud. The silver flesh of trout
glints in the river as they slide upstream
below stars that slip backwards from the lip
of the solar system, undetected, glowing like quasars.

And so, when I bend to kiss your cheek,
and stand in silence as you glide down that
easy sliproad into fire, I know one day
the sun will break out like a spilt egg,
engulf us, while neutrons pulse and cluster
and we're woven in a mesh of ice and rock
and hydrogen, become planets and protostars,
spinning comets swinging in new orbits.

The Other Side

Maybe she had gone there. She didn't know.
But what was certain was that she had changed.
The stem of her was hollow as a reed,
so words blew through her like a flute,
and her tears were icicles that snapped
before they reached her cheeks.

When she returned, each feather,
lighter than helium, drifted back to where
it had come from. The bone-nest
between her shoulders raw and cold
without that rooted wing-weight,
wind nudging the eyrie of her muscle.

She wanted to lift her arms again,
feel the current soar her upwards,
as she went higher and higher, energy
fizzing, a flickering light, everything fading
but the rush of air   taking her back

to the other side of somewhere

Fishing

You had to be quiet for the fish to bite. Orange twine held
firmly in small fists, feeling the nibble of each rising wave,

the trawl of light in our fingers. Often we'd catch a soft-backed crab,
twisting like an acrobat, pincers snapping at a clutch of air.

Sometimes I saw my father look to sea, salt like an enzyme
in his cells as he stood above us on the chalky cliff.

Mother baited the hook, plunging barbs into the heart of limpet,
soft hands slitting the pearly flesh. Patiently she'd wind

the paternoster, charming knots, removing kinks. Coiling
the twine like thick oiled wool, she made the pattern clearer.

On Swimming In A Fountain:
The Fountain Responds

This girl, who smells of wool and woodsmoke
and the faintest trace of perfume, has got inside me.
She swims carelessly, splashing me over the edge,
her arms thrashing. I take you into my body, girl,
the shimmer of your skin, the salty taste of you,
but would spit you out if I could.

I am no Rococo fountain, no mostra of Venice
or Milan. I have no goldfish in my depths,
no boy with dolphin clasped in carved arms,
Neptune with his trident jetting spray
or lions with their roaring open mouths.
No coins drop in me from passing strangers.

I am plain old stone. Fashioned for the time,
darkened with age. Algae moulds my corners,
slippery as caul. At night I dream of fine lights
illuminating me, women cooling themselves
with unfolded fans, peacocks milling round
my base with raucous, strident cry.

And yet this girl has slipped into my soul.
Her hands shiver like butterflies
below my curves, as if I'd birthed
her from a womb of stone.
She goes round me and I circle her endlessly,
flow through the caught web of her fingers.

She is a Naiad. I should marry her, were I a king,
and she my Melusine. I will keep the memory
of her printed in my atoms, remember
the warmth of her, even when I am drained
and full of leaves, my cracks and fractures hidden
under a cornice of bruising snow.

Penelope's Tale

The day he left, I started to uncurl
from the girl I had been, to a woman waiting
at the window for her husband's safe return.

He set out joyfully for Troy, his new mistress
creaking under her wooden stays, the veins
of her sails tense against the halyards,

sea beckoning like a siren. A purl of wind
filled the canvas, the trireme anxious
to be gone with her skirl of straining oars.

I had no need of heroes. Too young to be a widow.
I wanted to ask, who will tend the fire,
fetch in sacks of corn and wine, warm

to my flesh in the clasp of frost, fend off
unwanted suitors? My nagging filled his ears
like a scold of bees. Soldiers do not think

of the women left behind, how their skin
soon fades like apricots, their clear complexion
muddies in an ocean of angry tears.

Ten years on, Odysseus, the garden spoils,
the fields unploughed. My bloom has also gone,
that quick wit that you loved, my youthful blush.

I weave the endless days into a shroud.
Each sleepless night I unpick the threads,
walk the palace walls, imagine your ship

wrecked on sharp rocks, surf casting you
to land. Your men flung from the curved
black hull, tossed to a squall of waves.

My bed grows cold: and yet, new shoots appear
from the olive of its frame, ivory gilded
with leaves from the sprouting roots.

I want to weave myself out of this myth,
find you waiting at my hearth again,
the tang of sand and sea-salt on your breath.

Sea Symphony
After The Odyssey

Fish lip at the edge of foam,
blown mouths courting the salty water.

Their music is a low rush of tide,
soft as the slash of a knife through satin.

Spray brushes back from fins
as they swim the raw current. Underneath,

anemones reach up like chandeliers
hung from the ocean bed

and a snow of scattered light sifts
to the surface. Requiems of sea robins

drum and pulse a shanty: the crack
of icequake hollows still green chasms.

And here, mermaids. Sheering through the swell,
deft hands picking kelp or clam

eyes like dark soaked plums
and that dangerous song a thin hum

charming the swimmer and the sailor,
the seekers of rough water, those who cross

the perilous straits or fish from hand-carved
wooden boats, landfall too far for shelter.

How do these men survive the bellied tides,
the opened bag of winds that purl deep chords,

shake sail and mast and stern until
the shroud snaps and the sound trembles?

They fill their ears with softened wax
against the shredded music of the ocean,

the sough of whale and porpoise,
of turtle and frilled shark.

Half-mad, they grasp at the stolen sleep
of starfish, see the sallow ash of rain

falling on the surface, the feckless ghosts
of the dead rise from deep drowned places.

And the mermaids smile, unshackled
from the land, hair like filaments

of porphyra, floating, floating, arms calling
safe haven from the storm, leading the sailors

to the wandering rocks, the crash of breakers,
the unearthly scream of coral.

Saying Goodbye

for John

Not a station platform, but a harbour wall.
Waves oiling the slimy concrete,
the tide ebbing back
as you cast away the ropes,
slipped quietly out of my life.

By the time you come back, the sea will have changed you.
Firmed by the long blue jaw of water
and the shift of horizon,
you will be fixed to the sway of deck,
the four-hour watch, the pull of the helm.

You will have sailed over secret valleys
of sunstars, avenues where crabs
walk through sunken cities.
Over curls of sea horses, cruising squid,
marlin and amberjacks.

Your eyes will have turquoise in them
and the gloss of Atlantic sun.
There will be coral beneath your nails,
wrack and sea moss in your hair,
a crust of salt on your skin.

At night in bed, whales will call to you,
a deep sound like a cyan wind
singing through the trees,
and you'll be restless, tossing the pillows,
and I'll know it's gull and cormorant you long for.

When you return, I will bring you
the gifts of dry land, scents
of narcissus and summer lilac.
You will bring me shells,
a hollow conch,
the silence of the ocean in your fist.

Playing Chicken

A cautious boy. They called him 'chicken'
because he wouldn't be drawn into picking

the short straw, to dash on railway lines
or dart across the road for a childish dare.

He played the cello at school. His frail
uncertain fingers hesitant on the strings,

a long gold slur of chords burring round
the playground in the diffident heat.

Outside, girls skipping, the crump of tennis balls,
a laze of bees bumbling the dusty window.

He grew tall, strong armed, and wanted more
than Dvorak and Vivaldi, wanted to belong

to the boys who taunted his timid past,
yearned for excitement, the thrill of action.

No chicken now. A soldier sweeping mines,
detector held out rigid as a bow

in his steady hand, the weight of others' lives
pressed down on his young shoulders.

No chicken as he stepped onto the scrubland,
as his feathers unravelled, his wings flew,

and the hero of his blood scattered
like ghost-notes into the arid air.

Veteran

i.m. Neil Tierney, 1913-2001

Another day, and a coiled note of autumn,
the keen of rain on the glass.

My father, burly as a brown bear,
shambling down his garden,

planting his feet steadfast in the soil
as though doubtful of its firmness.

He has the cast of old scars printed on the yield
of his soul. Unable to forget the script of the past,

the unforgiving gristle of his dreams
sounding like gunfire on the cord of night.

He turns, pushes open the gate, and is surprised
by sun, weather, the amazing commonplace of things.

I think now of the truth of him,
the terrible load of memory.

How he carried it always like a sack of coal,
aching from its weight, unable to put it down.

The Man Who Wanted To Play The Violin

He dealt with love in that shy, dismissive way:
as if brushing a fly from his favourite coat,
shielding sun from the dusk of his eyes.
Walking into his study now, the dust is heavy
as osmium, curtains husked with age,
and the ghosts of forgotten notes hang
like dream-catchers in the silent room
weaving music into the fabric,
into long-unread poetry, pencil-scribbled scores.

This was a man who longed to play.
Whose fingers straddled the frets as easily
as a cranefly tremulous on a window pane.
He'd take the carefully-rosined bow, draw it
across the strings. Yet the sound refused to soar,
was grounded in arpeggios and broken chords.
His flawed music flurried through the house
like a rabble of butterflies, their wings
a thrum of raindrops, vivid crotchets.

I remember when his head began to slip
from the stave his life had moved along.
The words discordant, the sense jangled.
When the day became long fermatas
and he sat sipping tea, humming the opening bars
of Bruch, listening to the vibration of the stars.
Whilst I dealt with love in the only way I could:
playing him Oistrakh or Menuhin,
watching the sky turn, waiting for the coda.

A Rhetoric of Loss

Tonight I'm grieving for my language.
I stare at steam in the bathroom mirror
for letters I recognise – a message-
something beyond today
and its tired work-face,
the blurred vapour of water.

Today I'm grieving for my skin,
the new clammy softness of folds,
the fist that's now a thin grip,
flesh that creases like an unzipped dress.
For young cells shed carelessly
in an unremembered bed.

I'm grieving for rivers. For lost streams
leaked to sea, minnows dragged
from shallows by a mischievous flow.
I sorrow for the swallow blown off course,
the stones that are tumbled out of place,
shells washed up on the shore.

I'm grieving for my eyes.
For the sight of a hare purling
across a far field. The sharp heart
of thistle, a glance of sorrel,
edges unfocussed by a bitter wind.
For the stumble of words on a page.

The Pain Game

Tell me, Mr. Munch, on a scale of 1 to 10,
how bad is the pain? This slash of yellow
in the sky, is it a 4 or 9? And the swirling
gouache of blue, is this a 7 or a 2?

The man silently gapes from the frame.
The flay of his face held between
splayed fingers. Eyes wide, mouth open,
his head a burnished planet.

And when did the pain first appear?
Is it in your mind, or in the air? Does it fly
like a lark spinning on the wind,
what colours are the feathers of its wings?

Perhaps he will tell how the tempera
of the sunset gets inside your head,
a burning flash of pigment. How the soul cracks
like a shattered egg before the shriek of colour.

If he is able, he will describe the skew of it,
the slip-sideways gasp of it. How at night
it creeps up, slitting the dark's throat
as flesh seems to peel from your bones.

How that scream rises from the mouth of the earth
red as blood, as tongues of fire,
how the world is breaking on a brushstroke
sable-soft, infinite as despair.

Finding A King: Richard III

Curved spine, a sprinkle of bones
exposed beneath tarmac, the tyres
of Volvos and Fiestas. He had dreamed,
perhaps, of being laid in green fields
or sleeping away centuries
in the quiet grey stone of the friary.

He had not imagined the cloned sound
of cars droning above his shattered skull.
The chatter of workers, slammed doors
echoing down to cloister walls.
The fade and dissolve, one age to another,
transitioning time and faith.

All he knew was the smell of horse. The sweet
damp sweat, incense of dust and hay,
the pull of her between his legs.
The courser's breath flayed out in the heat of battle,
but she was steady, sound, carried his friendship
in her head among the clash of sword and lance.

He thought himself invincible that day
until his horse mired in the soft ground.
Pressed back against the marsh
tired with wounds and clamour
his circlet tumbled to mud as his blood ran free.

Slicing through rubble, mill waste,
he lies below the shade of Herrick's garden.
Such a slight skeleton
white against the red trenched earth.
A king raised from a shallow grave
still dreaming of victory.

Beachcombing

A sheep, slipped from the cliffs,
legs shattered, head a cave of stone.

Frayed rope, knotted stems of dulse,
the bleached dry husks of cuttlefish and urchin.

And you, driftwood, sitting with your back
to the ribs of slate, sleeping perhaps,

watching dogs sniff the smashed masks
of spider-crabs, muzzles grizzled with salt.

Rock drinking your shadow, half-eaten
by heat, you could be just a bundle

of abandoned kelp, a baked fall of clay,
a dredged-up chimera.

Picking Grapes

In remembrance of Kandanos, Kedros, Kondomari, Amari, Anogia: Crete

The village gathered for the harvest.
Picking ropes of glossy fruit,
the rich globes ripe and swollen.

Tossed onto coarse black nets
or into wicker baskets, donkeys cropping
on dried grass, half hidden by the vines.

The women would bring lunch. Cheese
and olives, almonds, wrapped in dark cloth
to keep them cool, jugs of sweet *Liakito*.

They worked in thick heat heavy with myrtle
and oleander, the smooth-skinned grapes
smelling of laurel, of wild forest honey.

And then the sound of marching on the still,
scented air. Army boots loud along the dusty track,
stained with fallen walnuts, pale fig blossom.

The grind of metal and latched rifles,
kri-kri leaping from rock to rock, geckos and skink
scattered from their basking walls.

The villagers frozen, as if time had ceased,
had framed their stooped, sudden poses
and the shock of stopped sound.

They dropped in the fields. Tumbled
in slow motion, packed fruit tipped
from the baskets. A stut of bullets

falling, falling, as if it would never end,
the black slump of bodies to the ground.
A spurt of smoke rising like early mist

to the mountain tops, as houses burned,
and children were taken from the razed walls,
shot in the shade of tamarisk and pine.

Olive trees swayed from the ricochet.
A glaze on the musky skin of bark and leaf,
juice staining earth, the parched soil parted.

The grapes next year blood-red, blooming.

The Lost Seal

*On 22.12.14, a grey seal swam from the Mersey estuary through a series of
streams and rivers, ending up in a field at Red Bank Farm, Newton-le-Willows*

Something like a memory drew him.
Away from the estuary and city lights
to brooks and meadows, where December
winds blow through sways of winter oak,
shake the swathe of grasses.

Sankey, Newton, Millingford, past
lost shells of cottage, factory, railway
arch and mill. He calls for his siblings,
misses the jostle of the herd,
bodies weaving through the current.

Only he knows that the sky is different,
his stars shifted from their compass.
At night the moon is too close, pastels
his coat with gold light, and he wants
the deep-dip cold of sea, arc of muscles

tensing down, that quick salt-rush
of wave, the swell of tide. He searches
for trout or salmon as he moves
through sedge and sweet flag,
stoneflies hovering above in a slow cloud.

He beaches in a field, crawls onto
grass-that-is-not-sand, air musked with
tilled earth, a sting of frost in his nostrils.
Cows stare amazed as he flippers over mud;
in his breath, the ghost of far oceans.

He leaves the stream to grieve him, scent
locked in its cells, the memory of his
body stored. Brought out one distant
autumn day, so that water will remember
that once, there was seal in its heart.

The Shibboleth of Blackbird

In his stern black feathers
he swifts from elm or sycamore
to claim his patch of seed.

His song drips into sluggish veins,
the fluency of music, as blackberries ripen,
dark and sleek as his body,

and rooks canvas the sky in late sun.
He chides the chough and jay who stray
into his territory. Feels the tightening

of light like a catch in the syrinx,
as evening unravels and dusk settles
down on fuschia and opening primrose.

This song is shared through generations,
a gift of merle, and he, proud of his heritage,
shouts it loudly from the branches,

from roof and chimney, heralds it
from blackthorne and rowan.
He offers this soliloquy to me,

the one who has stolen his land,
who does not sing the litany of dawn
or the last high notes of summer

but whose bread, hesitantly offered,
he takes as a mutual bond.

Aberglasney

Five maidservants died at Aberglasney in the C17th, supposedly after having been suffocated by lime plaster drying in their bedroom

Five ghosts are here. I see them
in the robin's eyes, in the wary haunch
of the squirrel. Five chattering girls,
their lime-filled breath stopped
like the wash of time across my mouth.
We walk through the ancient yew tunnel,
light round as a full moon at the end.

The house is falling around us.
Giant knotweed strides the garden;
a pile of lives rust by the door.
But on the hearth the robin stores his seeds,
and bramble curves the window-frame.
Your hand on mine a chasm, deeper than that drop
to the drowned dark cellars below.

A crashing through the undergrowth
startles us back three centuries. Skittering
to a halt, a baby deer, breaking her youth
on these nets of age. In her eyes I see
her fear: just as, waking for an instant,
I see those five girls draw their breath,
go wandering in their ruined flesh
passing through stone, brick, and the yew,
into landscape, indistinct as rain.

Footprints

The fossilised Happisburgh footprints, dating to the early Pleistocene, were
discovered on a beach in Norfolk, in 2013, and later destroyed by the tide.

Just for a tide's span the silt skinned back
to show these hollows, a print of human feet
preserved beneath the sand and shelly gravel.

Almost a million years since they strolled
along these mudflats, beside the estuary,
a graze of horse and elk in the river valley.

Walking among deer and bison, their soles
hard as iron on the tough heathland.
Arms full of treasure: crabs and shellfish, seaweed,

the saltmarsh treacherous underfoot.
Children with fistfuls of pinecones,
stooping to peer at a scurry of voles and mice,

the sudden dart of beetles in the scrub.
Adults testing flints, running sharpened edges
across their palms, wary of wolf and hyena

hidden in the shelter of the forest.
They startle at the call of crow and owl,
starling and ptarmigan, as evening draws down

and bullfrogs sound alarm across the reed swamps.
They shiver in a sting of winter cold
as harsh winds gust and the cooling sun

glints on water, on a sudden flip of sturgeon
in the river. Soil tightens into itself,
as if it had a memory of the coming ice.

The children scuff birch twigs along the ground,
making deep scores in mud. Not knowing
they are writing poems, drawing a Picasso.

The Creed of Cataloguing
Strata Florida

Perhaps the blood of a monk, he says
as he lays down the manuscript
with loving, white-gloved fingers.
We peer enthralled at the stained page
imagine Brother Cadwgan
kneeling to pray in the cloister.
The swift treason of a knife.

He catalogues the monks:
Brother Anian's neat letters
Rhydderch ab Ieuan's distinctive hand.
He searches for provenance,
skims through the rules of his order,
turns hierarchies to numbers, logical, precise.

He runs his fingers over the spine,
tooled leather, endbands,
codices gathered into quires.
He is a text-seeker, eager
to sink himself into litany or missal,
the musky echo of flesh,
lampblack, and salts of old ink.

He pictures five scribes
working with aching backs
in the dim scriptorium.
Transcribing annals, copying
breviary or psalm,
laying gold leaf on a ground of gesso.

And the poet, too,
buried by the abbey grounds
with his immaculate verses
still singing *cywyddau* in his head.
He too is classified, codified,
as he lies in the valley of flowers
under a twisted girdle of yew.

The Day The Water Walked
Aberaeron, 2014

This winter, seas and rivers have wakened.
Not wanting to be trapped on shores
by high chalk cliffs and barriers of stone,
the water is walking. Running, rushing
across promenade and town, it polevaults
over gates and railings, shoaling its way inland.

Listen to the silent cry of fish
open-mouthed in amazement
as they wash into streets and backyards,
swim through grass and winter heather
as sky flickers with wind, and seahorses
gallop and jump like wayward children.

The tide swells proudly over the pier,
batters thresholds, slips through
cracks and keyholes. Saltwater gathers
in carparks as shingle spreads into shops
and homes. A crush of shells and small shrimps
pool together on carpet and tarmac.

Cuttlefish flush into gullies: drains are filled
with featherstar and snakelock.
Anemones seed tentacles in garden beds,
their soft bodies rooting to stones
as sea hare nestle among sweet balm, slide
under the withered leaves of last year's planting.

An ocean away, the water has stopped mid-flow,
a candle of lace crocheted down rocks and falls
crystals delicate as lace. It is waiting its turn,
for the thaw from Arctic blast, the polar vortex.
One day they will join: the melted lakes
and the careless slurry of storms.
Harmonies of water, the merging of earth and air.
Fish swimming to the stars, becoming angels.

The Nest

We prized apart the stiff green bones
of euonymus. Arms scratched by twigs,
a shower of caterpillars spilling
to the ground. The inside of the bush
was dark, warm, tangy,
like the nave of a cathedral
ripped open to the sky.
A nest! he said, and lifted it out
in its woven wholeness.
Empty of eggs, but under our feet,
a smashed grail of shell.
I noticed how strong his hands were,
the clench of muscle.
Together we reached into the secret space
and our fingers touched.
I had thought we might find God in the shiny leaves.
I knew he was everywhere,
even in the heart of trees and black spaces
and the corners that couldn't be found.
He brushed my shoulder
dawdled his fingers down
to the bright dank hollows
of my new soul.
And I was lost
then and for all time
in a shimmer of bees,
the frail uncertain call of the fledgling.

Crow

Crow perches on the branch, a dark atheist.
Below, magpies hustle the ground for trash.

She watches him from the window
as he rowdies his way across the neighbourhood.

His nest is a pulpit of bones, from which he preaches
anarchy, as fledglings jangle bedlam from above.

The essence of him trampolines the grass,
saunters his way into sacks of morsels,

transmutes stones into food. She sees him dance
in the trees, rabble-rousing like a drunken man,

as she watches with hooded eyes, and the air breathes
only beaks, chaotic shapes, an alchemy of crow.

Remembering Capel Celyn: Liverpool, 1965

In our greed, we thought you didn't need
the water. The valley's bowl already blown with rain,
the surplus drained inside a soak of earth.

Yet sometimes, I could hear *dw'r* slip
silent into the sink, words slither down
the windows like a melt of winter ice.

Our valleys were the railway cuttings;
Edge Hill, Olive Mount, that slow slide into
Lime Street. Our fields were Sefton Park

and Calderstones. The city dragging on
its smoke, a gleam of sun splintering the sky,
the arcs of glass in the Palm House.

We had spoiled our water. The dredged river
dull and sullen – *glas*, you would say –
sheened with oil, blue as magpie feathers.

So we wanted your water like hiraeth,
bringing us the soft *glaw* of rain, scents
of sheep and meadow hooking our roots.

For we were Welsh too, our names cwtched
away by marriage, loved the hidden lyric
of our streets. Rhiwlas and Powis, Dovey,

Madryn, Wynnstay, Teilo, Gwent. Our
aunts with their secret handshake of vowels
behind those doors our heritage had closed.

A nain and taid too, with raw weather-skin
and roughened hands; how they'd sit
in the garden late on summer days

and long into evening, look towards the hills,
the heathered sky. *Come here, cariad,*
see Moel Famau, Snowdon, your mam-gu's land.

Your dead were drowned for us, bones
floated underground. Schoolbooks submerged,
their language sunk beneath the reservoir.

Now in our baths, larks' tongues sound,
the toll of chapel bell, a faint smell
of ashes doused inside the chimney stacks,

the *hwyl* of Sunday sermons. In our basins
are roofs, mossed stone, a chip of brick,
clanging from the pipes like angry ghosts.

Your water tumbles from our taps,
clear and sleek as a mountain stream,
tastes like an accusation on my lips.

Walking in Bronant

Softly on these late roads sun speckles
through like dapples on a Welsh mare.
A badger moon, striped with cloud, noses
autumn into the darkening sky
and a wind sharpened by September mist
shakes handfuls of sparrows from the oak.

Hazel, its branches looped from the ground
like a Menorah, lit by pale husks.
Brooches of clover embedded in stone,
ivy snaking rusty iron gates. Love-in-vain
twists through the ruins, unfurling
each morning, the flag of an old empire.

The dry remains of poplar lean against
the walls of a once-lush garden.
Here the chaffinch endlessly mourns,
and lacewings strum a delicate arc
above the blurred outlines of flowerbeds,
hover over a trace of silted river.

A buzzard's thin sostenuto layers along
the dust: crickets clack in yellowed grass.
The air is full of the must of pollen,
musky roses trapped in a fragrant past.
Our words shimmer like dragonflies
on the cusp of evening light.

Your blue dress is caught by the breeze,
your body held in a muffle of fabric.
And I remember how your heart howled
like a squall that last November.
Pulling up your roots, felling you,
the loss spiralling as blown leaves,
the scud of the owl's shrill cry.

Leaving

i.m. Pauline Daniels, 1945-2012

This is everything. The mouth of wind
in your garden, redwing and swallow
preparing for flight. Leaving hawthorne,
winter meadows, rowan berries
and harsh frost. The owl's riff
held in water like a memory.

You watching, eyes pennybright
as the blackbird, letting nothing pass you by,
not the ragged rasp of leaves,
the flicker of mice under sycamore.
The dark steal of night harvesting fox,
the sweep of a bat fresh from sleep.

And now my palm still remembers
your hand imprinted on mine,
that hot salt kiss on the shore of the ward
and the hem of you turned back
like an unstitched garment,
raw, unsure, at the border's edge.

The harsh alarm of the jay
scrimmaging for acorns
is silenced in this garden,
where the soft rot of apples and pears
is snatched by fieldfares for their journey.
And wind no longer pushes aside
the flapping ghosts of your Monday wash.

Evensong

While evening rooks are shrieking compline
the light is dying. The hot room tightens

and the earth is slipping through our fingers
as sun soughs along the ceiling, and the waiting

shrine their memories to this moment. Outside,
honeysuckle shadows the beech, and the rubble

of remembered walls. You have left a patrin
of breath behind, a handful of chanted whispers

and the last sigh of wind in the trees
ripples the bistort and tall reeds

like a footstep walking through them
when the evening is far spent.

In the branches the rooks break bread together.
Be sober, be vigilant, the storm is stilled.

Ice Music

In this cold snap, rivers are cracking under seams
of thick ice, streams unlearning the shapes they knew.

The moon is trapped in the pond, its alchemy of light
cupped in dense water, starlings sipping its edges.

Water is frozen in the throat of taps; bluetits peck
at smooth flutes of milk on the doorstep,

the blackbird's song hushed as gusts of snow
blow across the garden like a sheet of ghosts.

Newts and minnows slow as their world cools
and hardens, snails caught in the whitening rim.

The pool is locked, silent, but the ice is tuning up.
Already there's a humming in the air, a stiffening of tone.

Softly it comes, in days' lengthening. Sometimes
a high wire of sound, sharp as a whistle or piccolo,

or a slurred low vibrato, raw as a bassoon.
The moon begins to melt, lighting up fallen leaves,

the wait of nymph and goldfish. Lilies, chilled
like flowers in resin, quiver with the rhythm

of the notes. Tonight will be dark, moonshine sinking
to the bottom of the pool. And the ice is singing.

Vanishing Point: Venice

Here, the slow decay of water,
shutters and crumbling stucco,
soft lap on stone in hard-oiled light.

Lucid shadows, fragile as ormer shells,
a pearl gauze locking chiaroscuro
onto peeling walls, doors hennaed by sun.

Lizards, pale against chipped brick,
scud down to damp glazed pavements,
the surge of tide across the square.

Pigeons scroll through the air, writing
the sky with grey quills, perch on the cold
chipped fingers of marble statues.

Vaporettos coast the Grand Canal
like Stations of the Cross: landing stages
bob wildly in their wake.

In the cemetery, the dead are slipping
into water, quietly over the centuries;
cypress sit in a root-wash of waves.

On Poveglia, ruins roofed with branches,
windows trellised by vine and bramble.
Peach-trees grow in bone-rich soil,

haunted by the souls of ashed bodies
from the plague-pits, the ghosts
of doctors in long beaked masks.

This hiraeth of water remembers
merchant fleets- galere da mercato-
the shallow draft of galleys, sleek hulls

slipping through the locks: silks,
dyes, cloves and gold, spilling
like sacks of gems on the harbour wall.

It remembers the vedutista scumbling
paint on canvas, the scribbled purl of ships,
black gondolas straining like stallions

on their ropes. Everything is mirror,
reflection, the sfumato of cloud twinned
in early morning haze on the lagoon.

A city built on stilts, poled into salt-marsh
on alder and larch. A slow dissolve.
The water's lapse, the vanishing point.

And one day it will belong to grebe,
to night heron and egret, to tern
and cormorant, the tender eucharist of light.

Re-Entry: Apollo 11

It was the light we noticed first. Nearing earth,
we quickened to the pull of her horizons.
The curved burn of her rim shifted in the window
as we skimmed the radiation belts. Mountains
brailled across her surface, the swift flux
of her fist tilting us into her magnetic field.

We'd left behind the moon's bleak seas
and craters, our suits still covered in lunar dust.
Left the wastes of space, husks of cooling stars,
the dense exhausted core of white dwarfs.
Their stretched red glimmer receding
as we prepared to cross the Kármán line.

And then re-entry. Falling from orbit, we
breached the exosphere. Fire sleeked
from the heat-shield, shocked gas streamed
from the cone. Tight-knuckled, we prayed:
waited to melt, for titanium to be flayed back,
flesh turned to bone-ash as the capsule glowed.

Tumbling through musters of low cloud,
we brushed the planets off our spacesuits,
prepared for splashdown. Light came at our eyes
like a raven, pecking the stellar dark of retinas,
blowing pupils wide. It crept into visors
and pockets, the webbed dry of our fingers.

Splashing down to that ambush of ocean,
light years peeled into the swell, drogues
floating their tendrils on the water. A quiff
of wind rocked the capsule as we drifted
silently, handfuls of dusk gathering like fish
on the side, a gesso of last sun on the waves.

There are no words for it. That quiet moment
of repatriation, gravity hefting our bodies
with its sudden tug. Home. A breath of clean salt
bitter on our lips, recovery ships waiting,
and the deep quilt of galaxies now far above us.
We open the door. Drown in light.

Command Module
Apollo 11

They started to download her heart,
emptying her memory of distance, speed,
that terrible velocity. Charted solar wind
and moonquake, the sky's graffiti written on
her skin. They took our cargo of lunar dust,
sifted through disks of codes and figures,
rocks we'd scooped up from the lava-crust.
Wanting to strip those ancient, distant
myths: the moonshine. But the capsule,
still reeling in its star-struck head, might it not,
just for a moment, pause to remember
that tremble – unrecorded in its data banks-
an odd, uncertain flicker. Something outside
of itself, something it might call 'God'?

Red Kite

Above the cloisters of soil and shrub,
she hovers in her astonishing red,

wings scorching the air as she spools
across fields of sheaves and cut stubble.

Jackdaws spin like flecks of grey ash
girdle her with a jabber of black,

tugging the air with their loud complaint.
She tilts into the wind, her call a high frail

on the current, and her shadow falls across
the pond and the slow leat as she circles her heft,

a shawl of rain misting the hedges, the redshift
of her feathers quilled against the sun.

Above, a dissonance of stars, the suttee of day
fading into evening, moon unfolding its yellow eye.

Gate Fever

Each morning I put on the sky,
shrug the weather across my shoulders
like a shawl of softest wool.

The hasp of wind catches me by the throat
on this autumn day, huddles the lambs
into a quarry of hedge and their fleece honeys out
on the brambles like strands of pollen.

They are clouds on legs, a scurry of cumulus.
Rams barging the ewes for shelter,
damp coats smelling of meadowsweet in the rain.

Like them, I fear to go too far from my own heft.
Beyond the fence a hunch of mountains
heavy and wet with drenched slate,
roads that lead to unfamiliar places.

Today the gate is unlatched, and a quiet voice
calls home the sheep from their rooted pastures.
We stand and watch, amazed, as the mouth
of the world is opened: the slow unravelling of lives.